LAST STAND
AT THE ALAMO

LAST STAND AT
THE ALAMO

ALDEN R. CARTER

Franklin Watts
New York/London/Toronto/Sydney
A First Book 1990

For the Tollefsons

Many thanks to all who helped with Last Stand at the Alamo, *particularly the staff of the Marshfield Public Library; my editors, Marjory Kline and Reni Roxas; my mother, Hilda Carter Fletcher; and my friends Barbara Jean Feinberg, Don Beyer, Dean Markwardt, Jim Alexander, and Joyce Meinders. As always, my wife, Carol, deserves much of the credit.*

Cover painting courtesy of: *Texas State Archives*

Maps and illustration by Joe LeMonnier

Photographs courtesy of: Texas State Archives: pp. 6, 16, 25, 38, 53, 56, 57, 60; Barker Texas History Center: p. 11; Texas State Capitol: pp. 14, 20, 35; Institute of Texan Culture: pp. 29, 43; Daughters of the Republic of Texas Library: pp. 30, 41, 51; Texas Highways Magazine: p. 46; New York Public Library Picture Collection: pp. 48 (both), 55, 58

Library of Congress Cataloging-in-Publication Data

Carter, Alden R.
Last stand at the Alamo / Alden R. Carter.
p.   cm. — (A First book)
Summary: A brief look at the battle of the Alamo, an event which was instrumental in procuring Texas's independence from Mexico.
ISBN 0-531-10888-0
1. Alamo (San Antonio, Tex.)—Siege, 1836—Juvenile literature.
[1. Alamo (San Antonio, Tex.)—Siege, 1836.   2. Texas—History—To 1846.]   I. Title.   II. Series.
F390.C316   1990
976.4′03—dc20   89-22688   CIP   AC

CONTENTS

Lieutenant Colonel William Barret Travis, commanding officer of the Alamo garrison in its last days

1
THE ROAD TO THE ALAMO

Lieutenant Colonel William Barret Travis was in no hurry as he rode toward the Alamo. That was unusual because the tall, red-haired Travis had been in a hurry most of his twenty-six years. Travis was a very ambitious man, and he wanted a glorious role in the fight to win independence for Texas. Yet this February day in 1836 found him leading only thirty men toward the tumbledown Spanish mission in the dusty town of San Antonio de Bexar. Travis could see no fame or glory lying ahead, but the road he traveled so unwillingly would lead into the pages of history.

Like most of the men who rode with him, Travis had lived only a short time in Texas. He had been born in 1809 on a farm in the backcountry of South

Carolina. When he was nine, his large family moved to Alabama, where his father hoped to buy more and better land. Early in life, Travis decided that he wanted no part of farming. At the first opportunity, he moved to the up-and-coming town of Claiborne to study law. By the age of twenty, he had taught school, begun a law practice, and founded a newspaper. He was married, the father of an infant son, and seemed on his way to becoming one of the state's leading citizens.

Then something went terribly wrong. The most widely believed story is that Travis's wife starting carrying on with a gambler and that Travis killed the man. Whatever the exact details of his troubles, Travis found it wise to leave Alabama in a hurry. He headed for Texas—that vast, underpopulated land where a man could easily lose an unpleasant past.

Texas was then part of Mexico, which had won its independence from Spain in the early 1820s. The Spanish Empire had never encouraged settlement in Texas, viewing its emptiness as protection for the rich provinces farther south. In Texas, the Spanish flag flew over a handful of lonely missions where a few soldiers guarded Franciscan missionaries trying to convert friendly Indians to Christianity. Beyond the missions lay the unsettled distances of Texas.

There the Comanches roamed—a powerful tribe of expert horsemen, buffalo hunters, and warriors. The Spanish might have claimed the land, but the Comanches were the true lords of Texas.

Spain's empire had once included all the land between the Mississippi River and the Pacific Ocean. But in 1800, the French dictator Napoleon forced Spain to hand over the land drained by the great river. In 1803, Napoleon sold this vast area, then called Louisiana, to the young United States for the amazingly low price of fifteen million dollars.

The Spanish distrusted their new neighbors, whom they called *norteamericanos,* or North Americans. And the North Americans gave them plenty of reasons. Frontiersmen trapped and hunted in Texas without permission. Military exploring parties from the east pushed deep into the unsettled lands before Spanish soldiers turned them back. Spanish spies in New Orleans and Washington brought news of North American plots to invade Texas.

The Spanish saw that Texas needed law-abiding settlers loyal to Spain. When a Missouri businessman, Moses Austin, offered to start a colony of hardworking families, the Spanish government quickly agreed. Moses Austin died in 1821, leaving his son Stephen to carry out his dream. That same year, the Mexican people rebelled against their Spanish rulers. Two years of war led to the founding of the Republic of Mexico.

The new Mexican government welcomed Stephen Austin, giving him a huge area of Texas to sell to settlers for as little as four cents an acre. Within a few years, there were a number of North American colonies in Texas. In exchange for a few hundred dollars and the promise to become a Mexican citizen and a Roman Catholic, a settler could buy more land than he'd ever dreamed of owning.

Many settlers tried to be good Mexican citizens, but others refused to pay taxes or to obey Mexican laws. Some smuggled in goods and slaves from the United States. In 1826, settlers around the town of Nacogdoches went so far as to declare the independent state of Fredonia. Loyal citizens led by Austin put down the Fredonia Rebellion, but the Mexican government grew increasingly worried.

By 1830, North Americans outnumbered the native Mexican citizens of Texas by at least three to one. The Mexican government saw Texas slipping from its control. It ordered a halt to further settlement by North Americans, put tight controls on trade with the United States, and sent more troops to Texas to enforce the laws. Austin and others objected to the new rules but were ignored. Most of the new Texans simply ignored the rules.

Advertisements such as this rallied people in the United States to the cause of Texan independence.

William Barret Travis arrived in Texas in the late spring of 1831. He set up a law practice in the small port town of Anahuac and took an immediate interest in local politics. He soon tangled with the town's military governor, a hard-bitten soldier named John Bradburn, who had worked for the Mexican government since the revolution. Colonel Bradburn had little patience for the complaints of his fellow North

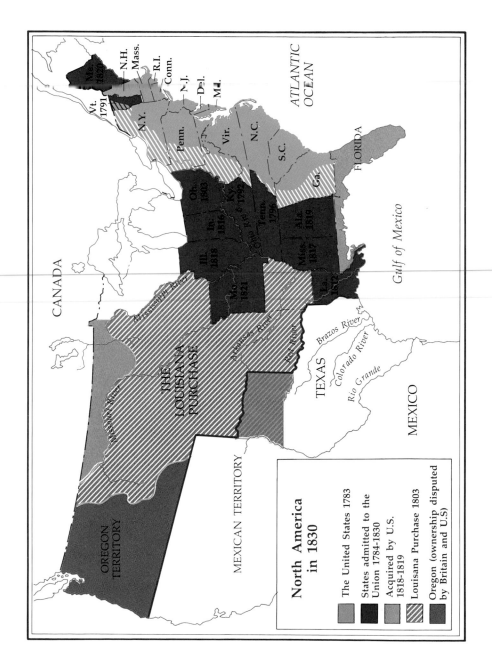

North America in 1830

Legend:
- The United States 1783
- States admitted to the Union 1784-1830
- Acquired by U.S. 1818-1819
- Louisana Purchase 1803
- Oregon (ownership disputed by Britain and U.S)

CANADA

ATLANTIC OCEAN

Me. 1820
Vt. 1791
N.H.
Mass.
R.I.
Conn.
N.Y.
N.J.
Del.
Md.
Penn.
Vir.
N.C.
S.C.
Ga.
FLORIDA

Ohio 1803
Ind. 1816
Ill. 1818
Ky. 1792
Tenn. 1796
Ala. 1819
Miss. 1817
La. 1812
Mo. 1821

Ohio River

THE LOUISIANA PURCHASE

Mississippi River
Missouri River
Arkansas River
Red River

OREGON TERRITORY

MEXICAN TERRITORY

TEXAS

MEXICO

Brazos River
Colorado River
Rio Grande

Gulf of Mexico

Americans. On the first excuse, Bradburn arrested Travis and another lawyer named Patrick Jack and tossed them in jail.

Angry citizens demanded the release of the two men. Bradburn refused. News of the arrests spread, and a small army of North Americans gathered. One of Bradburn's Mexican patrols was captured and held hostage. Citizens trying to bring two cannons to Anahuac traded fire with a Mexican outpost. Bradburn's superior stepped in just in time to stop really serious trouble. He replaced Bradburn and set Travis and Jack free.

After little more than a year in Texas, Travis was a hero to many people. He became a leader of the so-called War party, a group favoring independence for Texas. The War party saw Texas's future linked with the United States, not Mexico. Opposing Travis and the War party were Austin and his Peace party, favored by most North American and Mexican residents of Texas. The Peace party saw a future where Texas would be a largely self-governing state within a united states of Mexico.

At that time, Texas was part of the Mexican state of Coahuila, which had its own problems and paid little attention to Texas. Austin and his followers wanted a separate state government for Texas. The Peace party pinned its hopes on Mexico's strong-

Stephen F. Austin founded the first colony of English-speaking settlers in Texas and saw Texas's future linked with Mexico, not the United States.

man, General Antonio López de Santa Anna, who was trying to bring peace to the country after a decade of troubles. In the summer of 1833, Austin set out for Mexico City. He hoped to persuade General Santa Anna to ease the new rules on settlement and trade, and to let Texas form its own legislature and court system.

Santa Anna seemed to listen at first, but then began putting off the Texan's requests. Austin vented his frustration in a letter that fell into the wrong hands. Santa Anna slapped him in prison. Texans were outraged by the news of Austin's arrest, but fear for his safety kept them from taking up arms.

As the months of Austin's imprisonment wore on, the War party grew impatient. Late in June 1835, Travis decided it was time for a bold move. With twenty-five men, he seized Anahuac, capturing the town's small garrison. Travis expected this action to spark a revolution, but he misjudged the mood of his fellow Texans. Travis was loudly criticized. Many towns sent messages of loyalty to Santa Anna. Travis and the War party were disgraced.

A wiser man than Santa Anna might have taken the opportunity to improve relations with the Texans. Instead, he ordered General Martín Perfecto de Cós to take a strong force into Texas. Cós was to arrest Travis and the other troublemakers, crush further unrest, and get the Mexican laws working

The Mexican dictator Santa Anna sent an army under General Martín Perfecto de Cós (shown at right) to put down the rebellious Texans.

once and for all. Santa Anna's harsh orders were too much for most Texans. Almost overnight, the mood in Texas swung in favor of a war for independence. When Stephen Austin finally returned home in early September, even he favored revolution.

In late September, General Cós occupied the provincial capital of San Antonio de Bexar. The first real fighting took place in the small town of Gonzales, seventy miles to the northeast. Some of General Cós's troops tried to seize the town's cannon. They were met by Texans flying a flag bearing the taunt,

Come and Take It. Both sides hesitated for two days, then clashed on the morning of October 2, 1835. A shot from the town's cannon scattered the Mexicans. They fled back to Bexar.

A ragtag army of North Americans led by Austin marched on Bexar to throw General Cós out of Texas. Austin's army surrounded the town, then settled down to wait for more men. Among the arrivals was Travis, who was given command of a small band of scouts.

Meanwhile, representatives from all over Texas met in San Felipe for a "consultation." They formed a government, made the army official, then decided to send Austin to the United States for money and volunteers. To command the army, they chose a former army officer and governor of Tennessee, Sam Houston. The towering Houston was a good choice, but the Consultation gave him little support. Its members fell to bickering. For months they would argue over the aims of the revolution and the details of organizing the new government.

At Bexar, the Texas volunteers grew restless. Tired of inaction, Travis left for San Felipe. Finally, on December 5, a weathered plainsman named Ben Milam took matters into his own hands. At the head of 240 men, he stormed into the town. Milam died in the bitter house-to-house fighting, but his men pressed forward. On December 9, General Cós surrendered. He was allowed to take his men back across the Rio Grande on condition that they would not fight in Texas again.

With Cós defeated, many of the volunteers thought the war was won and headed home. Most of those who still wanted action set out to capture the rich port of Matamoros in Mexico. Colonel James Neill, a dedicated but unimaginative officer, was left at Bexar with few supplies and less than a hundred men. Without the means to defend all of the town, Neill ordered his men to make a fort out of the old Spanish mission on the far side of the San Antonio River. It would soon become world famous as the Alamo.

Built in 1718 by Franciscan missionaries, the Alamo was originally named the Mission of San Antonio de Valero. The Franciscans left in the 1790s, and the soldiers who remained began calling it the Alamo. *Alamo* means cottonwood tree in Spanish. Cottonwoods may have grown nearby, but more probably the soldiers chose the name because they had once been stationed in a Mexican town called San Carlos del Alamo de Parras.

For most of its nearly 120 years, the Alamo had slumbered under the Texas sun. But those quiet days were drawing to a close.

2

MAKING A STAND

William Barret Travis and his thirty dusty men arrived at the Alamo on February 3, 1836. He reported to Colonel Neill and was surprised to find Colonel James Bowie with him.

Bowie had arrived in January with instructions from Houston to destroy the Alamo and bring its cannons east to the Brazos River, where Houston was trying to raise an army. Houston did not want to risk either men or valuable weapons defending Bexar against the large army Santa Anna was raising to recapture Texas. But Bowie had liked the cut of Colonel Neill's North American and Mexican volunteers and liked even more the strong walls of the old mission. He advised Neill to ignore Houston's orders and make a stand at the Alamo.

Colonel James Bowie,
"the most dangerous
man alive," helped
defend the Alamo.

Jim Bowie was not a man to run from Santa Anna or anyone else. At forty, the big, sandy-haired Bowie was one of the most famous fighters on the frontier. Born in Kentucky, Bowie grew up on the Louisiana bayous, where he made a name for himself as a hunter, logger, and riverboat man. When he was twenty-three, he and a brother lit out for Texas. On Galveston Bay, they fell in with the famous pirate Jean Lafitte. They bought slaves from Lafitte and smuggled them into Louisiana, investing their profits in land deals of doubtful honesty. Life on the fringes of the law brought brawls and duels aplenty. Bowie's favorite weapon was a long, ferocious knife with a double-edged point. The knife became known far and wide as the "bowie knife" and its owner, Jim Bowie, as "the most dangerous man alive."

Despite his rough-and-tumble life, Bowie was no ruffian. Courteous and generous, he was invited to the best homes in New Orleans. Eventually, however, his shady land deals caught up with him. In 1828, he moved to Texas, beyond the reach of sheriffs and lawsuits. He fell in love with the beautiful daughter of the Mexican vice-governor. They married and lived happily together until 1832, when the young Mrs. Bowie and their two children died in a cholera epidemic. Bowie never fully recovered from the loss. He drank heavily and his health began to slip. But war revived the fighter in him, and he readily threw in with his fellow Texans.

Both Bowie and Travis were strong-willed men. They would differ on many things in the coming weeks, but they agreed on the need to defend Bexar, the only really important town in West Texas. Between the Rio Grande and the Brazos, there was little to stop or even slow the Mexican army except the old mission at Bexar. The Alamo had not only thick walls but twenty cannons, the largest collection in Texas. With enough men and gunpowder, Bowie and Travis were sure they could hold the Alamo almost forever. Let Santa Anna waste his soldiers trying to capture the Alamo while Sam Houston raised an army to win independence.

At the center of the Alamo was a plaza about the size of one and a half football fields with stone walls nine to twelve feet high. Along the inside of the walls ran low buildings that had once housed Spanish soldiers, their workshops, guardhouse, and kitchens. Beyond the barracks on the east side was a walled corral. Set back from the plaza's southeast corner was the chapel. Its walls were strong, but the roof had caved in years before, leaving only a few small, protected rooms still usable. General Cós's troops had built a platform for three cannons atop the east side of the chapel.

The weakest point in the Alamo's defenses was the fifty-yard gap between the end of the plaza's south wall and the chapel on the east. To fill the gap, the Alamo's engineering officer, Captain Green Jameson, built a log-and-earth wall called a palisade. Jameson strengthened other walls and built more platforms for the Alamo's cannons. At the southwest corner, eight hundred yards from the center of town, he mounted the Alamo's biggest cannon, an

The Alamo

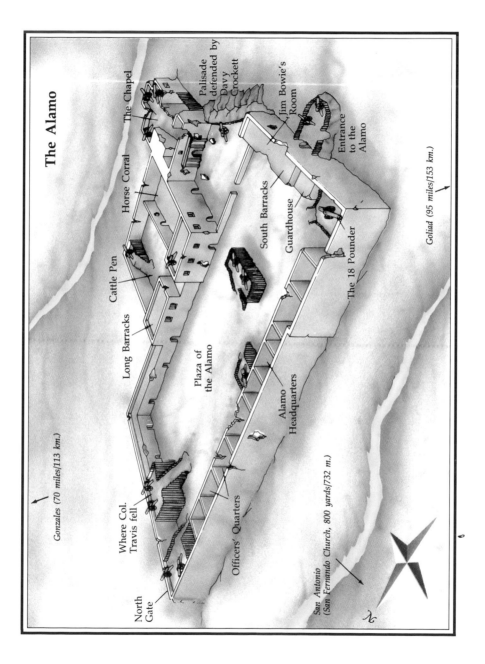

Gonzales (70 miles/113 km.)

Where Col. Travis fell

North Gate

Officers' Quarters

Long Barracks

Cattle Pen

Horse Corral

The Chapel

Plaza of the Alamo

Palisade defended by Davy Crockett

Jim Bowie's Room

Entrance to the Alamo

South Barracks

Guardhouse

Alamo Headquarters

The 18 Pounder

Goliad (95 miles/153 km.)

San Antonio (San Fernando Church, 800 yards/732 m.)

N

eighteen-pounder. The cannons of the day were rated by the weight of the solid cannonballs they could fire at fortifications or distant infantry. Against charging infantry, they fired many smaller balls, called grapeshot, or even rocks and scrap metal.

But cannons and stout walls could not make up for the Alamo's great weakness: it was simply too large for so few men to defend. With the arrival of Bowie and Travis, Neill had about 140 men. The number grew by another thirteen on February 8 when Davy Crockett rode into the Alamo with his Tennessee Mounted Volunteers. The defenders of the Alamo turned out to give a rousing welcome to perhaps the most famous frontiersman in America. Crockett delivered a rip-roaring speech that set everyone cheering. Santa Anna might have his thousands, but the Alamo now had Davy Crockett.

At fifty, Crockett had been a bear hunter, pioneer, Indian fighter, and—most recently—a politician. He had been elected to Congress three times, using his backwoods humor and easy way with words to become a national figure. For a time, he followed the lead of his old friend Andrew Jackson, who became president in 1828. But Crockett could not stomach Jackson's harsh policies toward the Indians and the poor settlers of the frontier. He broke ties with the popular president and lost his seat in Congress in the fall election of 1835.

Frontiersman, politician, and yarn-spinner, Davy Crockett led his Tennessee Mounted Volunteers in the fight at the Alamo.

[25]

Angry with the voters, Crockett packed his bags and headed for Texas with several friends. At almost every town along the way, he was hailed as a hero. More men joined him, earning places in the Tennessee Mounted Volunteers, even though most had never even seen the state. Some people thought Crockett's journey to Texas was just a stunt to give him publicity for another stab at politics, perhaps even a run for president. But it seems that the sight of the Texas plains—open and wild as far as the eye could see—swept away any thought Crockett had of returning to Washington. He told the men of the Alamo that Texas was now his country and that he desired no greater honor than to fight for its independence as a simple soldier.

On the night of February 10, the men of the Alamo threw a lively party, called a *fandango* in the Southwest, for Crockett and his "Tennesseans." It was past midnight when one of the Alamo's Mexican scouts rushed in to tell Colonel Neill that Santa Anna's army was approaching the Rio Grande, only 150 miles from Bexar. The officers discussed the report and decided that it could not be true. No one expected the Mexican army until spring brought better marching weather and new grass to feed the army's horses. The party went on.

Colonel Neill lacked any real enthusiasm for defending the Alamo. The next morning he departed on leave, never to return. Travis, as the senior regular army officer, took command. Trouble arose almost immediately. Only a few of the men at the Alamo had actually enlisted in the regular army of Texas. The rest were volunteers, like Bowie and Crockett. Bowie, a colonel of volunteers, was unwilling to take orders from the younger and less experienced Travis. The volunteers demanded the right to vote on a leader, forcing Travis to call an election. Bowie won by a landslide, leaving Travis in command of only the thirty regular soldiers who had accompanied him to the Alamo.

To Travis's disgust, Bowie and his men spent more time in town than working on the Alamo's defenses. Crockett, who also held the title of colonel, liked both men and refused to take sides. Finally, Bowie and Travis came to an uneasy truce by agreeing to act as joint commanders, both signing all reports and orders. Slow, peaceful days settled on the Alamo.

The defenders wouldn't have been so relaxed had they known that the scout's report had been correct. On February 16, Santa Anna led his army across the Rio Grande into Texas. The Mexican army was a mixed lot. Many of its men were raw recruits or homesick Indians. Santa Anna had even emptied the jails to swell the ranks of his army. But there were also well-trained, experienced troops, particularly the cavalry in their gleaming breastplates, the tough infantry veterans, called *grenadiers*, and the *Zapadores*, or fighting engineers.

At forty-two, Santa Anna was energetic, brave, often brilliant, and always ruthless. He had risen rapidly in Mexican politics, making and unmaking governments until he became president in 1833—the first of five times he would hold the office in his long and stormy life. Fancying himself "the Napoleon of the West," Santa Anna cared little for anything except his own power and wealth. His soldiers suffered terribly on the long march through the deserts and mountains of northern Mexico. The army had no doctors for the sick or priests for the religious. Few of the men received warm clothing or enough food. Yet their general drank his wine from a crystal goblet and ate rich meals served on fine china and silver.

While Travis and Bowie continued to ignore reports brought by friendly Mexicans, Santa Anna's army marched on toward Bexar. On February 21, it was only twenty-five miles from the town. A group of frightened townspeople visited Santa Anna's camp. They told him that the Alamo's defenders were holding yet another *fandango* that night. Santa Anna ordered General Ramírez y Sesma ahead with

General Antonio López de Santa Anna,
dictator of Mexico

The defenders of the Alamo first heard reports of the Mexican army's approach during a fandango— *a dancing party popular in Texas.*

the cavalry to surprise the Texans and take Bexar without a fight. But a flooding river blocked Sesma's way, and the cavalry had to wait through the next day for the water to go down.

On the morning of February 23, Travis was astounded to see hundreds of Mexican families fleeing Bexar with their possessions piled on carts, horses, donkeys, and their own backs. He demanded to know what was going on, finally learning that the

Mexican cavalry was only miles away. Still unwilling to believe that Santa Anna had arrived so soon, Travis ordered a lookout to climb the steeple of the San Fernando Church.

At one o'clock in the afternoon, the lookout started ringing the church bell furiously. Travis rushed up the steep stairs but could see nothing but empty prairie. The lookout swore that he had seen cavalry but that they now lay hidden behind a low hill. Travis sent two volunteers, Dr. John Sutherland and John W. Smith, to have a better look. If they found Mexican troops, they were to return at the gallop.

The lookout watched the two riders trot into the afternoon haze. They seemed to pause, then suddenly they swung their horses about and raced for town. A squad of Mexican cavalry hurtled over the hill in pursuit. Sutherland's horse fell, then scrambled to its feet. Smith turned back and helped the injured doctor remount, then together they dashed toward the safety of Bexar and the sound of the bell pealing the alarm.

There was great hubbub in the streets by the time the two men reached town. Soldiers and townspeople rushed about, grabbing weapons, food, and blankets. Soon a stream of men, women, and children were hurrying toward the Alamo on the far side of the San Antonio River.

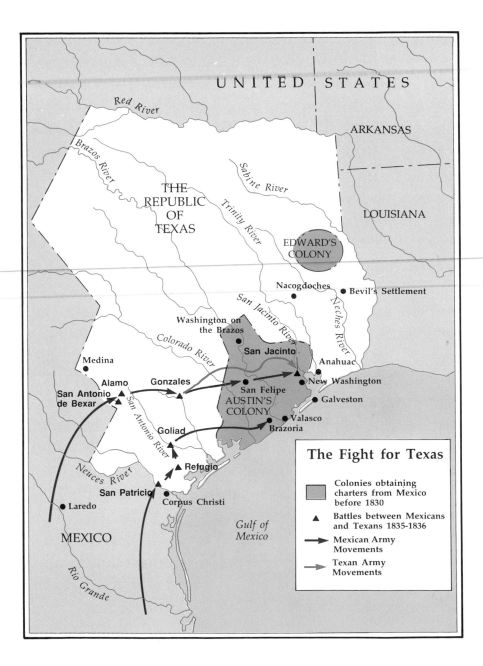

UNITED STATES

ARKANSAS

Red River

Brazos River

THE
REPUBLIC
OF
TEXAS

Sabine River

LOUISIANA

Trinity River

EDWARD'S
COLONY

Nacogdoches ● ● Bevil's Settlement

Neches River

San Jacinto River

Washington on
the Brazos

Colorado River

San Jacinto

Anahuac

Medina ●

Alamo

Gonzales

San Felipe

New Washington

San Antonio
de Bexar

AUSTIN'S
COLONY

Galveston

San Antonio River

Goliad

Valasco
Brazoria

● Refugio

Neuces River

San Patricio ●

Corpus Christi ●

● Laredo

Gulf of
Mexico

MEXICO

Rio Grande

The Fight for Texas

Colonies obtaining
charters from Mexico
before 1830

▲ Battles between Mexicans
and Texans 1835-1836

→ Mexican Army
Movements

→ Texan Army
Movements

Despite his injured leg, Dr. Sutherland volunteered to join Smith in riding the seventy miles to the town of Gonzales for help. A young man named Johnson offered to take a message to the Texans at Goliad, ninety-five miles to the southeast. Travis scribbled notes begging for supplies and men. Crockett approached. "Colonel, here I am. Assign me to a position, and I and my twelve boys will try to defend it." Travis gave the Tennesseans responsibility for the Alamo's weakest point, the palisade at the southeast corner of the plaza.

Two hours later, the Mexican cavalry, with Santa Anna now in command, rode into Bexar. Spurs and harnesses jangled, and the sun glinted from swords, lances, and polished breastplates. As the defenders of the Alamo watched, a blood-red flag unfurled from the steeple of the San Fernando Church. It carried the fearful message that Santa Anna would take no prisoners. For a long moment, a hush seemed to hang over the afternoon, then the Alamo's prized eighteen-pounder roared. The Texans had given their answer.

3

VICTORY OR DEATH

The roar of the Alamo's big cannon rolled over the plains, overtaking the messengers riding hard for help. A man headed for the Alamo also heard the distant thunder. Lieutenant James Butler Bonham was on his way back from delivering a message to Fort Defiance at Goliad. He did not have good news for his friend Travis.

Bonham and Travis had known each other as children in South Carolina. They grew to manhood in different states, but their paths crossed again when Bonham arrived in Texas late in 1835. The dashing, handsome Bonham was a man after Travis's own heart; neither of them could resist the thrill of an adventure. Bonham became Travis's most trusted friend.

Lieutenant James Butler Bonham galloped through Mexican lines to reach the Alamo.

A week before Santa Anna's arrival in Bexar, Travis had sent Bonham to Goliad with a request for reinforcements. But Bonham was unable to convince Colonel James Fannin to send any of his more than four hundred men. Now the sound of the cannon told Bonham that the Alamo's defenders would soon need all the help they could get. He set spurs to his horse and dashed for Bexar, sweeping past startled Mexican soldiers and through the gates of the Alamo.

After hearing Bonham's disappointing report, Travis set about writing more pleas for help. Across the San Antonio River, more Mexican soldiers flooded into Bexar. They began mounting cannons and digging trenches to encircle the Alamo.

The next morning Jim Bowie could not rise from his bed. After weeks of fighting off illness, the most dangerous man alive lay tossing with a raging fever. No longer able to continue as joint commander, he handed over all authority to Travis. That afternoon, the Mexican cannons began hurling shells into the Alamo. Amazingly, no one inside was killed. The Alamo's guns replied only now and then, since the Texans had little gunpowder to spare. The Mexicans stopped firing after dark. Then, to the astonishment of the Texans, the roar of cannon fire was replaced by music. With grim humor, Santa Anna had ordered his band to serenade the defenders of the Alamo.

In his small office, Travis picked up his pen and wrote:

To the People of Texas & All Americans . . . I am besieged by a thousand or more Mexicans under Santa Anna. . . . The enemy has demanded a surrender. . . . I have answered . . . with a cannon shot. . . . I call on you in the name of Liberty . . . to come to our aid. . . . If this call is neglected, I am determined to sustain myself as long as possible & die like a soldier who never forgets what is due to his own honor & that of his country—Victory or Death.

Over the next few days, the Mexican trenches lengthened. Every day exploding shells fell into the mission and solid shot shook its thick walls. At night, Mexican raids tested the Alamo's defenses. During the day, Mexican sharpshooters fired from the cover of tumbledown shacks nearby. The Texans struck back, torching the shacks and picking off any Mexican unwise enough to show himself within rifle range.

Travis watched the horizon for some sign of approaching help. He had sent Captain Juan Seguín, the leader of the Alamo's Mexican volunteers, with a message to Houston. Other messengers darted through holes in Santa Anna's lines with appeals to the Texans at Gonzales and Goliad. Travis knew that help must arrive before the ring of trenches closed around the Alamo, leaving his 150 or so men to stand off Santa Anna's mighty army alone.

The weather, which had been unusually warm for mid-winter, turned nasty. Rain and a cold north wind swept the old mission. Night after night, the Mexicans fired cannons or blew bugles to keep the tired defenders from getting more than snatches of sleep. When Bowie could find the strength, he left his room to encourage the men. Davy Crockett joked, told stories, and did everything he could to keep up their spirits. He found an old fiddle and

Captain Juan Seguín led the Mexican volunteers at the Alamo. After delivering a plea for help to General Houston, he returned too late to share the fate of his friends. In later life he became one of Texas's most respected citizens.

challenged a bagpipe-playing Scot to a musical duel. More than a few Mexican soldiers must have listened in confused wonder to the resulting din from the Alamo.

On February 28, Travis again sent Bonham to Goliad to plead with Fannin. Travis did not know it, but Fannin had set out for the Alamo two days before. But a cart broke down, the oxen strayed, and the men grumbled about bad luck and low supplies. The timid Fannin took the first excuse to turn around. His men were safely back inside Fort Defiance by the time Bonham arrived. Fannin refused to march a second time.

The men of Gonzales had more courage. Alerted by Dr. Sutherland and John W. Smith, thirty-two men—all the men in town but one—took up their rifles, kissed wives and children good-bye, and set out for the Alamo. Smith led them through the Mexican lines in the early morning hours of March 1. Of this brave party, only Smith would leave the Alamo alive.

Two days later, Bonham returned. By then, the Alamo was completely encircled. Swearing to "report the result of my mission . . . or die in the attempt," Bonham plunged through the Mexican lines. Not one of the surprised Mexicans got off a shot. The last of the Alamo's defenders had arrived.

Travis refused to believe that Texas could be so deaf to his pleas. That night, he sent John W. Smith off with another appeal for help. Many of the men sent letters to their families with Smith. Travis wrote to the guardian of his young son: "Take care of my little boy. . . . If I should perish, he will have nothing but the proud recollection that he is the son of a man who died for his country."

The Mexican cannons hammered at the Alamo for two more days. On March 5, the Texans watched as Santa Anna's soldiers built ladders for scaling the walls. An attack was coming and very soon. In a lull in the firing that night, Travis called his exhausted men together. Bowie was carried from his room on a cot.

Travis surveyed his men. None were professional soldiers. Instead, they were farmers, ranchers, craftsmen, lawyers, teachers, and laborers. Except for Seguín's Mexican volunteers, few had deep roots in Texas. They had come to this land from eighteen different states and a half dozen foreign countries. All had been willing to fight for Texas. Now Travis needed to know if they were also willing to die for it.

He explained that his pleas for help had failed. If any man wanted to escape before the Mexicans attacked, no one would criticize him. He, however, intended to stay and sell his life as dearly as possible. Legend has it that he then drew his sword and scraped a line in the dust. Who would cross the line to stand with him? Only one man refused. Louis Rose, a French trader and soldier of fortune, saw no profit in dying for Texas or anything else. That night he slipped over the wall and fled.

Travis decided to send one last call for help. Bent low over his saddle, sixteen-year-old Jim Allen dashed into the night. Travis inspected his defenses,

*Colonel Travis's speech to his men on
the evening before the final battle,
as imagined by a 19th-century artist*

then took time to visit the twenty or so women and
children huddled in the chapel. Two were Mexican
sisters-in-law of Jim Bowie, others the wives and
children of Mexican volunteers. The only North
American woman was Susannah Dickinson, the
young wife of Captain Almeron Dickinson, the
Alamo's artillery officer.

Travis talked quietly with the women. He gave several of the children small presents. Finally, he slipped a gold ring with a black cat's-eye stone from his finger, tied it to a piece of string, and hung it around the neck of a 15-month-old Angela Dickinson. Then he was gone into the darkness for a last look at the defenses. At midnight, Travis and most of his men turned in for a few hours' sleep.

In the Mexican camp, Santa Anna told his officers the plan of attack. Four columns would charge the Alamo at first light. Two columns of about 350 men each would hit the northeast and northwest corners. Another force of about 300 men would try to get into the Alamo through the walled corral on the east side. The smallest column, about 100 men, would attack the southeast corner where the Tennesseans manned the palisade between the south wall and the chapel. Santa Anna would hold 400 crack troops in reserve to throw into the battle at the critical moment.

Some of Santa Anna's officers were unhappy with the plan. Why attack when they could starve and shell the Alamo into surrender? One officer wrote in his diary: "Why is it that Santa Anna always wants to mark his triumphs with blood and tears?"

At five o'clock on the morning of March 6, 1836, the Mexican bugles sounded the attack. With a

On the morning of March 6, 1836, the Mexican army charged the Alamo from all sides. The Texans drove back two attacks, but the Mexicans broke through on the third.

shout, the Mexican infantry charged across the two hundred yards of open ground to the north of the Alamo. The officer on watch, Captain John Baugh, ran across the plaza, yelling, "Colonel Travis! The Mexicans are coming!"

Sword and shotgun in hand, Travis raced toward his position beside a cannon on the north wall. "Come on, boys," he shouted. "The Mexicans are upon us and we'll give them hell." Passing some of Seguín's Mexican volunteers, he called out "¡No rendirse, muchachos!" ("No surrender, my friends!")

Along the walls cannons roared, tearing great holes in the charging Mexican columns. Rifles cracked, felling Mexican soldiers by the dozen. Leaping over the bodies of the fallen, the Mexicans pressed on against the hail of lead. Soon they were at the walls, trying to raise their scaling ladders. Travis leaned over and fired both barrels of his shotgun. A Mexican bullet caught him in the head, pitching him backward against the wheel of a cannon where he lay dying.

The heavy Texan fire forced the attackers back on all sides. The Mexicans regrouped and charged again. Over the din of battle came the sound of Santa Anna's band playing the *Deguello,* the traditional music announcing that no prisoners would be taken. Again the furious Texan fire broke the charge.

The Mexican soldiers were nothing if not brave. Again they gathered themselves and rushed the walls. The two columns attacking from the north pushed in together. Forced to slide to the right by fire from the corral, the column attacking from the east joined them. Santa Anna hurled his four hundred grenadiers and *Zapadores* into the crush of men trying to scale the wall.

Inside the Alamo, men abandoned their posts on the west and east to rush to the north side of the plaza. For fifteen terrible minutes, the fight raged at the north wall. With most of their ladders lost in the first two attacks, the Mexicans tried desperately to find another way to scale the wall. The Texans fired down into the heaving mass of men, killing and wounding scores. But the Texans had to lean far over the wall to aim their rifles, and Mexican sharpshooters began picking them off.

As the defense weakened, a few Mexicans clawed their way up and over the wall. The fighting became hand to hand, and the Texans began to give way. A Mexican reached the small gate inside the northwest corner and threw back the bar. A torrent of Mexicans poured through. Those Texans who could break free of the fight fell back across the plaza.

Almeron Dickinson rushed in to the chapel. "Great God, Sue, the Mexicans are inside the walls!" He embraced his wife. "If they spare you, save my child." He had no time to say more. He raced back to his post atop the chapel, as his gunners swung their cannons around to fire into the flood of Mexicans surging across the plaza from the north.

*In hand-to-hand fighting,
the Mexicans overwhelmed the
last of the Alamo's defenders.*

Suddenly, Mexicans were swarming over the south wall, too. The smallest of the four columns had attacked Crockett's Tennesseans manning the palisade, then slid to the left to hit the southwest corner. There they surprised the gunners of the Alamo's prized eighteen-pounder. In moments, the Mexicans were inside the plaza and shooting down the Tennesseans from behind. Several Mexicans raced to the main gate and threw it open. More soldiers poured into the Alamo.

The plaza became a chaos of hand-to-hand fighting. Without time to reload, the Texans fought with rifle butts and bowie knives against the bayonets and swords of the Mexicans. One Mexican account says that Crockett died near the south wall. Another says that he found shelter in the long barracks along the east wall.

Atop the chapel, Bonham and Dickinson were still firing their cannons into the plaza. Mexicans at the southwest corner wrestled the big eighteen-pounder around and blasted the Texans off the roof. Above the barracks by the corral, the Alamo's flag fluttered down and the flag of the Republic of Mexico shot up the pole.

The last of the Alamo's defenders barricaded the doors of the barracks and fired on the Mexicans from windows. The Mexicans blasted open the doors with

cannons, then charged into the smoke to stab, club, and shoot the dazed Texans. Bowie died on his cot, firing his pistols, then swinging his famous knife. Mexican soldiers smashed through the doors of the chapel, killed the few defenders, then shot down the two oldest boys among the terrified women and children before a Mexican officer stopped the killing.

Slowly the firing died away. Santa Anna rode into the Alamo to claim his triumph. As his officer had predicted, it was marked with blood and tears. The dead lay strewn from the north wall, across the plaza, to the south gate. In the hour and a half of fighting, nearly all the Texans and perhaps two hundred Mexicans had been killed, and at least another four hundred Mexicans wounded. In the shade of the barracks and the chapel, soldiers nursed terribly

Top: Davy Crockett's (dressed in brown) final hours as imagined by one artist. Bottom: Jim Bowie (wielding his famous two-edged bowie knife) did not fight as shown but died in his bed, too ill to rise for the final battle.

injured comrades. But without doctors, many of the wounded would die.

General Manual Fernández Castrillón approached Santa Anna, leading a half dozen bloodied Texans captured in the barracks. Many historians believe that one of them was Davy Crockett. Castrillón had given his word that they would be fairly treated, but Santa Anna refused to honor the promise. While the horrified Castrillón watched, Santa Anna's staff officers drew their swords and hacked the men to death.

The women and children were led out of the chapel. Santa Anna sent them to his camp. Two of the Alamo's men also survived: Travis's black slave, Joe, and one of Seguín's men, who convinced Santa Anna's soldiers that he had been held in the Alamo against his will.

Santa Anna ordered the bodies of the Alamo's 183 defenders burned. A Mexican family from Bexar pleaded for their son's body. Santa Anna allowed them to take it away for burial. Mexican soldiers stacked Texan bodies between layers of brushwood—Travis, Bowie, Crockett, Bonham, Dickinson, Jameson, the courageous men of Gonzales, Seguín's brave Mexicans—all those who had valued freedom more than life. That afternoon, a dark column of smoke rose into the Texas sky.

Santa Anna ordered the execution of nearly all the male defenders of the Alamo but spared the women and children. This painting, titled The Execution of Lt. Dickinson at the Alamo, *is historically inaccurate.*

4

REMEMBER THE ALAMO!

Santa Anna let the women and children go a few days later. On March 13, Susannah Dickinson arrived in Gonzales with Travis's slave, Joe, and another black man from Santa Anna's camp. Sam Houston had arrived to rally the Texans of the area and heard Mrs. Dickinson's sad tale of the last hours at the Alamo. He held her hand and wept.

Houston did not have enough men to stop Santa Anna. The Texans would have to run first and fight later. That night the Texans began what they would call the "Runaway Scrape." With Houston's tiny army hurrying them along, the North American residents of West Texas fled east. Among them were the some thirty widows and hundred fatherless children of Gonzales whose menfolk had given their lives at the Alamo.

Susannah Dickinson, shown here as an aging woman, was a young wife when her husband was killed at the Alamo. Released by Santa Anna, she gave General Houston an account of the last stand at the Alamo.

Fresh from his victory, Santa Anna divided his army, sending columns to crush the remaining resistance in West Texas while he pursued Houston with the main force. Near Goliad, General José Urrea caught Fannin's troops trying to escape. Surrounded, the nearly four hundred Texans surrendered. At dawn on March 27, they were marched to a nearby wood and shot.

Houston retreated across the Colorado River, then beyond the Brazos. Many of his men wanted to stop running and fight, but Houston knew what he was doing. His army gained strength with each new recruit while Santa Anna's army, divided and tiring, lost strength with each day. At last, on April 19, Houston turned to fight. He addressed his men: "Victory is certain! Trust in God and fear not. And remember the Alamo!"

The battle took place two days later at Buffalo Bayou on the San Jacinto River. Santa Anna had about 1,150 men, Houston fewer than 800. In the morning, the two armies tested each other. Hours of quiet followed. Santa Anna and his men settled down for a peaceful afternoon, confident that the Texans would not attack their larger army. At four o'clock, with shouts of "Remember the Alamo!", the Texans smashed into the Mexican camp.

The Battle of San Jacinto lasted eighteen minutes. Houston's men killed some 600 Mexican soldiers and captured nearly all the rest at a cost of only eight killed and 23 wounded. Santa Anna was discovered hiding in some tall grass the next morning.

A man of towering height and courage, General Sam Houston commanded the army of Texas.

Texas won its independence in
a crushing victory over Santa Anna's
army at the Battle of San Jacinto.

The day after the Battle of San Jacinto,
a humiliated Santa Anna (center, carrying dark hat)
was brought before the wounded Sam Houston.

More than a century and a half after the battle,
the Alamo still stands as a symbol of freedom.

He was held prisoner until the Mexican government agreed to grant independence to Texas in the fall of 1836.

Texas became the Lone Star Republic with Sam Houston as its president. On December 29, 1845, Texas became the twenty-eighth state of the United States of America. The story of the Alamo and its defenders became part of the national history. Captain Juan Seguín, who had returned too late to share the fate of his friends, said of them: "They preferred a thousand deaths rather than surrender." Today, more than a century and a half later, the words "Remember the Alamo!" still ring in the hearts of all who love liberty.

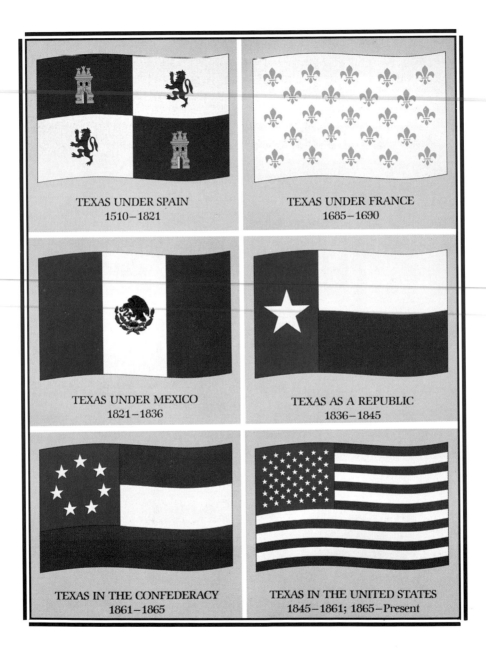

TEXAS UNDER SPAIN
1510–1821

TEXAS UNDER FRANCE
1685–1690

TEXAS UNDER MEXICO
1821–1836

TEXAS AS A REPUBLIC
1836–1845

TEXAS IN THE CONFEDERACY
1861–1865

TEXAS IN THE UNITED STATES
1845–1861; 1865–Present

SUGGESTED READING

Holmes, Jon. *Texas: A Self-Portrait.* New York: Bonanza Books, 1985.

Johnson, William. *Sam Houston: The Tallest Texan.* New York: Random House, 1953.

Lord, Walter. *A Time to Stand.* New York: Harper & Brothers, 1961.

"Texas Sesquicentennial Issue: Texas and the Alamo." *American History Illustrated,* March 1986.

Tinkle, Lon. *Thirteen Days to Glory.* New York: McGraw-Hill, 1958.

Warren, Robert Penn. *Remember the Alamo!* New York: Random House, 1958.

INDEX

ABOUT THE AUTHOR

Alden R. Carter is a versatile writer for children and young adults. He has written nonfiction books on electronics, supercomputers, radio, Illinois, Shoshoni Indians, the American Revolution, the Battle of Gettysburg, and the People's Republic of China. His novels *Growing Season* (1984), *Wart, Son of Toad* (1985), and *Sheila's Dying* (1987) were named to the American Library Association's annual list, Best Books for Young Adults. His fourth novel, *Up Country*, was published in 1989. Mr. Carter lives with his wife, Carol, their son, Brian Patrick, and their daughter, Siri Morgan, in Marshfield, Wisconsin.